Wilson Trail

Of the four long-dist[...] it is the Wilson Trail which sees the greatest var[...]on in surroundings. From the reservoirs of Hong Kong Island, and slopes above the densely-populated districts of east Kowloon, it extends across windy highlands to the northern edges of the New Territories.

David Wilson was the last governor to arrive wearing the colonial regalia later rejected by his successor, Chris Patten. Wilson's five years in office were marked by rancorous disputes with China over the financial and electoral arrangements for the impending handover, but also by an economic boom and record levels of investment by Hong Kong businesses in China.

The most auspicious day of the century – the eighth day of the eighth month of 1988 – was chosen to top off the Bank of China's angular new headquarters in Central. But fortunate feng shui and buoyant stock markets did nothing to dispel popular discontent with one-party rule on the mainland. Students and activists gathered to protest in cities across China. The following summer, the world was appalled by the Tiananmen Square massacre in Beijing.

In Hong Kong, panic set in as fears arose that China would repudiate the terms of the 'one country, two systems' agreement. Residents scrambled for foreign passports. Wilson announced the building of a new airport on Chek Lap Kok — together with gigantic earthworks, suspension bridges, railways and roads, the largest civil engineering project in Hong Kong history — to restore confidence and stem the wave of emigration. This achieved, he left office in 1992.

The end of the Wilson Trail is marked by a memorial to Edward Youde, the governor preceding Wilson. Fluent in spoken and written Chinese, he had previously been Ambassador to China and was perfectly suited to lead the complex handover discussions. Driving himself ever harder, he was found dead in bed after a heavy evening of negotiations in Beijing. He, like David Wilson, had done his best to secure a stable future for Hong Kong.

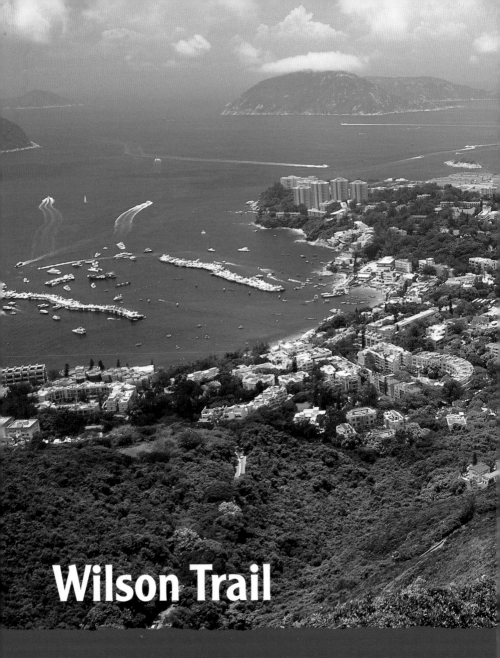

Wilson Trail

When you set out to walk the Wilson Trail, you embark upon a journey from edge to edge of Hong Kong, from the southern shore to within sight of the Chinese border. It's the only trail to make use of public transport – an MTR tunnel – to take hikers across

the harbour. The route takes in some of Hong Kong's best vantage points in Jardine's Lookout, Devil's Peak, and the Pat Sin Leng range of mountains, and covers great expanses of high, windy country far removed from the city clamour.

	Stage	Route
	Stage ❶ **Stanley Gap Road** 赤柱峽道	Stanley Gap Road 赤柱峽道 > Wong Nei Chung Reservoir 黃泥涌水塘
	Stage ❷ **Wong Nei Chung Reservoir** 黃泥涌水塘	Wong Nei Chung Reservoir 黃泥涌水塘 > Yau Tong 油塘
	Stage ❸ **Yau Tong 油塘**	Yau Tong 油塘 > Tseng Lan Shue 井欄樹
	Stage ❹ **Tseng Lan Shue 井欄樹**	Tseng Lan Shue 井欄樹 > Sha Tin Pass 沙田坳
	Stage ❺ **Sha Tin Pass 沙田坳**	Sha Tin Pass 沙田坳 > Tai Po Road 大埔公路
	Stage ❻ **Tai Po Road 大埔公路**	Tai Po Road 大埔公路 > Shing Mun Reservoir 城門水塘
	Stage ❼ **Shing Mun Reservoir** 城門水塘	Shing Mun Reservoir 城門水塘 > Yuen Tun Ha 元墩下
	Stage ❽ **Yuen Tun Ha 元墩下**	Yuen Tun Ha 元墩下 > Cloudy Hill 九龍坑山
	Stage ❾ **Cloudy Hill 九龍坑山**	Cloudy Hill 九龍坑山 > Pat Sin Leng 八仙嶺
	Stage ❿ **Pat Sin Leng 八仙嶺**	Pat Sin Leng 八仙嶺 > Nam Chung 南涌

Distance in km	Duration	Challenge
4.8	2.00	Strenuous hiking
6.6*	2.50	A fairly challenging walk
9.3	4.00	A fairly challenging walk
8.0	3.00	Strenuous hiking
7.4	2.50	Easy rambling
5.3	2.00	A fairly challenging walk
10.2	4.00	Easy rambling
9.0	4.00	Strenuous hiking
10.6	4.50	Strenuous hiking
6.8	2.50	A fairly challenging walk

total **78**

* Additional 4.5 km of MTR portion

Shenzhen

Sha Tau Kok

Lo Wu

Sheung Shui

✕ LO WU

✕ LOK MA CHAU

✕ SHEUNG SHUI

Fan Kam Road

Sha Tau Kok Road

LUNG YEUK TAU
LUEN WO HUI
Fanling
TONG HANG
Tsz Tong Tsuen
BIRD'S HILL

Fanling Highway

Kau Lung Hang
Lo Wai

NAM WA PO
TAI HANG
Wai Tau Tsuen
HANG HA PO
FONG MA PO

PAK TAI TO YAN 480m ▲
TAI TO YAN 566m ▲
PAK NGAU SHEK
TAI YEUNG CHE
TIN LIU HA
SHE SHAN
NG TUNG CHAI
LIN AU

Lam Kam Road

WUN YIU

95

KAM SHAN
✕ TAI PO MARKET

Island House

Tai Po

Tai Po Industrial Estate

Tolo Harbour

KUK PO
FUNG HANG
LUK KENG

Bride's Pool Road

Sir Edward Memorial
Ha Tsat Muk Kiu

NAM CHUNG
LO LUNG TIN
135
FINISH

Pat Sin Leng Country Park

Hok Tau Reservoir

110
115
▲ PING FUNG SHAN
WONG LENG
▲ PAT SIN LENG 120
LAI PEK SHAN ▲
130

Sha Lo Tung

Fung Yuen
Lo Tsuen

SAM TAM LO
CHUNG MEI
CHUNG PUI
125
TAI MEI TUK
PAT SIN LENG
10

Plover Cove Country Park

Plover Cove Reservoir

CHEUNG PAI TUN

Shuen Wan Hoi (Plover Cove)

PO SAM PAI
SAN TAU KOK
TING KOK
WONG YUE TAN
SHUEN WAN
SHA LAN

Ting Kok Road

TIN SAM

CLOUDY HILL ▲
9
105

SHUI WAI
Hong Lok Yuen
100
Tolo Highway

Stanley huddles around its bay, now enhanced by Blake Pier.
The trail beacons ahead

Wilson Trail

STAGE

1

Stanley Gap Road
赤柱峽道

Stanley Gap Road 赤柱峽道 >
Wong Nei Chung Reservoir
黃泥涌水塘

4.8 km / 2 hours

WONG NEI CHUNG GAP RESERVOIR
黃泥涌水塘

②

HK Parkview

Tai Tam Country Park

Wong Nei Chung Reservoir

▲ **VIOLET HILL**
433m

Tai Tam Intermediate Reservoir

TSIN SHUI WAN AU

▲ **CHEUNG LIN SHAN**
344m

▲ **LO FU SHAN**

THE TWINS

Repulse Bay Beach

▲ **STONE HILL (MA HANG SHAN)**
268m

Repulse Bay Road

South Bay

1 START

STANLEY GAP ROAD
赤柱峽道

Ma Hang Estate

Stanley

Stanley Bay

❯ Starting at Stanley Gap Road

Board any of buses 6, 6A or 260 at Exchange Square in Central. Alight between Repulse Bay and Stanley, after the bus has passed the right-hand turning for Chung Hom Kok Road. The correct spot, just above Ma Hang Prison, is marked by a mapboard.

There is little time to get acquainted with the Wilson Trail before it embarks on a stiff ascent due north. A total of 1,000 monotonous concrete steps lead up to the first lookout point on Stanley Mound. There's no need to pack a calculator, as some helpful soul has done the counting beforehand and announced every 100th step in neatly painted white numerals. At the lookout, you'll be glad of the excuse to stop and catch your breath. An engraved viewing compass provides an explanation of the vista laid out before you: Stanley, Chung Hom Kok and Repulse Bay; Tai Tam Harbour; and offshore, the sea-struck cliffs of Po Toi, shadowed by Chinese islands on the horizon.

Upwardly mobile – or down and out

Climb another 300-odd steps to marker *W002*. The Twins, not a mediocre Canto-pop duo but a pair of hills with equal musical talent, appear ahead on your line of travel. The minor rises off to your right have Chinese names very different from their English ones — Bridge Hill is Water-Lily Well Hill, for instance, while Sugar Loaf and Notting Hill are Tiger Hill and Tortoise Hill respectively. There are lovely views over Repulse Bay, the Tai Tam Peninsula and the all-embracing South China Sea.

Bays face south to bathe in sun

The trail crosses the Twins and then descends by way of a long flight of steps (left) to the Tze Kong Bridge at Tsin Shui Wan Au, or Repulse Bay Pass. Shaded paths branching off to the left lead back to Stanley and downhill to Repulse Bay. Carry on straight ahead, up a frankly uninspiring concrete staircase, to tackle Violet Hill — following the ridge as it curves west, then north, to approach the summit. With thousands of monotonous steps constructed in a misguided desire for safety, much of the natural charms of stages 1 and 2 of the Wilson Trail have been blighted.

Couched in the valley – Tai Tam Intermediate

Again the ascent entails over 1,000 steps, with a brief respite at *W006* where the sand path evens out. From this viewpoint high above the Tai Tam Reservoirs (left) you're able to look out at hills stretching north towards Quarry Bay. This high ground was the scene of the most decisive battles of the 1941 invasion, the defending forces eventually being pushed back by Japanese invaders towards the Stanley peninsula. From *W007* onwards, it's a breeze downhill.

Parkview is now visible (below), overlooking the small Wong Nei Chung Reservoir. The path passes between them to reach the road and the end of this section. If you're carrying on to Stage 2, you can stock up on drinks at the large supermarket here. Parkview has no public transport however, so if you are finishing here, you must walk downhill to Wong Nei Chung Gap, where buses can be picked up for Central and other points in town.

Wong Nei Chung and the city beyond

Skirting Stanley Mound

A crested Bulbul and Azalea blossoms add colour to Parkview

Southern shores: Deep Water Bay

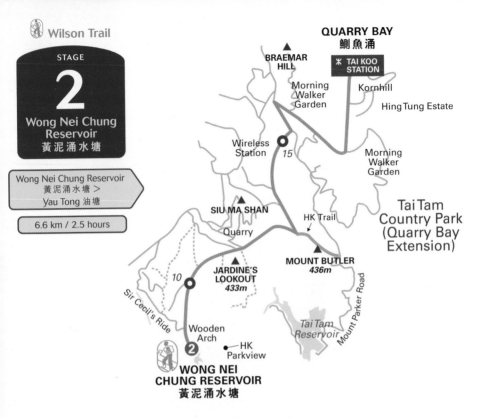

Wilson Trail

Wong Nei Chung Reservoir
黃泥涌水塘 >
Yau Tong 油塘

6.6 km / 2.5 hours

QUARRY BAY
鰂魚涌

BRAEMAR
HILL

✱ TAI KOO
STATION

Morning
Walker
Garden

Kornhill

Hing Tung Estate

Wireless
Station
15

Morning
Walker
Garden

Tai Tam
Country Park
(Quarry Bay
Extension)

SIU MA SHAN

HK Trail

Quarry

MOUNT BUTLER
436m

JARDINE'S
LOOKOUT
433m

10

Sir Cecil's Ride

Mount Parker Road

Tai Tam
Reservoir

Wooden
Arch

2

HK
Parkview

WONG NEI
CHUNG RESERVOIR
黃泥涌水塘

> ## Starting at Wong Nei Chung Reservoir

Take buses 6 or 66 from Exchange Square through Wan Chai to Wong Nei Chung Gap. Get off at the Hong Kong Cricket Club and walk ahead to the petrol station, turning left up a flight of steps to Tai Tam Reservoir Road. Walk uphill to Parkview.

Archway to two main trails

The start of the trail is impossible to miss – a wooden archway opposite the main turning into Parkview. This entry point to Tai Tam Country Park is shared with marker *H052* of the Hong Kong Trail, and sees a lot of pedestrian traffic.

Here there is also a sombre black-marble memorial in honour of the Winnipeg Grenadiers: a reminder of Canada's costly contribution to the defence of Hong Kong during the Second World War.

Verdant vista: folded landscapes of hills and water

Jardine's Lookout: The Wilson Trail offers a different perspective on the densely developed city.

W012 Headed north to new horizons

A flight of 275 steps leads up to the barren ridge of Jardine's Lookout. It's unlikely that William Jardine ever hiked up here himself, since he left the China coast before Hong Kong was founded; but his business partner James Matheson once owned a house on this hill, the ruins of which can still be seen. It is indeed a good lookout, offering unusual views across Happy Valley to Central (following spread), and certainly would have overlooked Jardine's original godowns at East Point – now better known as Causeway Bay.

Descend eastwards past the quarry towards Mount Butler, taking care to turn sharply left about 200 metres after *W012* in order to leave the Hong Kong Trail behind. The path continues over the summit of Siu Ma Shan (Pony Mountain) to achieve a panorama of the densely-packed northern shore of the island. The residential high-rises of North Point give way to striking views of the harbour and the Kowloon hills.

Jardine's Causeway Bay in quieter days

Cross the little bridge at *W015* and turn right, passing the masts of the Braemar Hill wireless stations to descend by way of stone steps into welcome greenery. Here, at the T-junction with a sandy path, the trail turns left to join Sir Cecil's Ride for a short distance. It has something of a spiritual aura, with makeshift shrines (opposite), smoke rising from incense coils and the hypnotic chant of Buddhist prayers emanating from concealed audiotapes. As the trail joins the road, bear left and then immediately right, passing under the Quarry Bay Tree Walk arch in the direction of Kornhill – not continuing on Mount Parker Road as you might assume.

This green hillside above Quarry Bay is very popular with elderly morning walkers, and facilities such as rain shelters and tables have been placed for their benefit. Plans to build another housing estate high on Mount Parker Road seem to have been shelved for the time being.

Between *W016* and *W017*, two outdoor wartime relics are preserved. Here field stoves were built on the northern slopes of Mount Parker, as a precaution after the October 1938 occupation of Guangzhou by Japanese forces. Threatened by the nearby presence of enemy troops, the government prepared for a siege, and readied first aid services, air raid advice

W016 Bamboo shrine to Kwun Yam

and a food rationing system. However, Hong Kong fell to the invading army after only 18 days of fighting and the two field kitchens (below) were never put into service. Today, local horticulturalists have filled in the wok burners, and turned them into blooming flowerpots.

W017 Woks alfresco: wartime field stoves on Mount Parker

High altitude over Happy Valley

Reservoir waters descend gently towards Tai Tam Bay

Bougainvillea brightens the route of morning walkers

Continue walking on toward the second open-air kitchen. On the right at the far end, the path descends into greenery, signposted to Kornhill. The trail finally hits urban Greig Road at *W018* where – contrary to the signpost, you turn left for the MTR – and follows it downhill to Quarry Bay. This busy residential district was for many years the site of the Swire dockyards (right, upper) and sugar refinery; in fact the name of the major development, Tai Koo Shing, means 'Swire City'.

Turn right onto King's Road for the short walk to Tai Koo MTR station. The road is also served by tram and numerous bus routes.

Taikoo Docks: Dry-docks attention for steamships of the day

W014 Eastern Edges: Quarry Bay and the Lei Yue Mun passage

Diverging trails: high above Quarry Bay

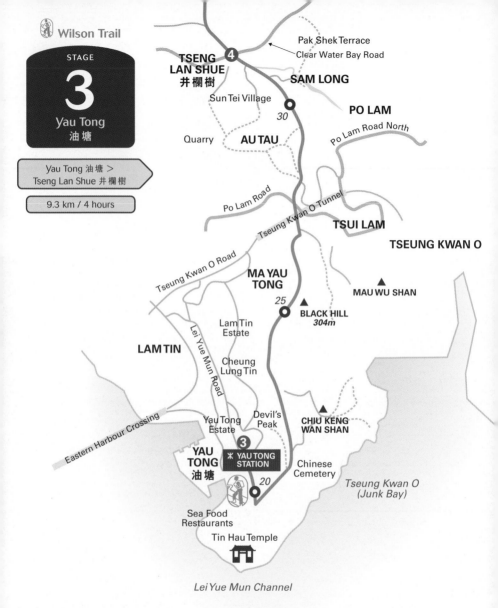

Wilson Trail

STAGE 3
Yau Tong 油塘

Yau Tong 油塘 >
Tseng Lan Shue 井欄樹

9.3 km / 4 hours

TSENG LAN SHUE 井欄樹

SAM LONG

Pak Shek Terrace
Clear Water Bay Road

Sun Tei Village

30

PO LAM

Po Lam Road North

Quarry

AU TAU

Po Lam Road

Tseung Kwan O Tunnel

TSUI LAM

TSEUNG KWAN O

Tseung Kwan O Road

MA YAU TONG

25

MAU WU SHAN

BLACK HILL
304m

Lam Tin
Estate

LAM TIN

Lei Yue Mun Road

Cheung Lung Tin

Devil's Peak

CHIU KENG WAN SHAN

Yau Tong
Estate

Eastern Harbour Crossing

YAU TONG 油塘

3 ✳ YAU TONG STATION

20

Chinese Cemetery

Tseung Kwan O
(Junk Bay)

Sea Food Restaurants

Tin Hau Temple

Lei Yue Mun Channel

❯ Starting at Yau Tong

There is as yet no bridge over the narrow Lei Yue Mun strait and, perhaps surprisingly, our mandarins have not proposed one, despite the fact that this no longer lies along the final approach to the former Kai Tak Airport. The Wilson Trail thus depends on transportation through the Eastern Harbour Tunnel to reach Kowloon side.

The official directions advise you to go to Lam Tin MTR station, leave by Exit A, and start from there. However, since the opening of the Tseung Kwan O Line, it is more convenient to start from Yau Tong station. This removes the need to walk alongside the traffic-choked main road, and allows an initial detour through the harbourfront shanty of Lei Yue Mun.

Ladies lazing: art on the MTR

Leave Yau Tong station by Exit A2, passing artist Li Wen-han's 'Fat People' installation on your left, and take the steps on your right down to Cha Kwo Ling Road. Follow the pink signs to Lei Yue Mun Seafood District. Keeping the stinky typhoon shelter on your right, walk through the gateway and the slippery labyrinth of seafood stalls, restaurants and village playground, bearing left at the shipping beacon to pass the public bath house. Just before you reach the village's Tin Hau Temple, the first trail sign appears, embedded in the concrete path, pointing your way up granite steps. As if to make up for lost time, trail markers appear every ten paces from this point on.

W021 Looking back across the Lei Yue Mun passage

Bear left once the path reaches the quiet road which leads to the Chinese Permanent Cemetery, and look out for marker *W020* clearly signposted on the opposite side. Here you must ascend a set of steps which heads uphill into the trees. This is also part of the Kwun Tong Fitness Trail. It's a relief to find you're on the right path and have escaped the oppressive embrace of the city below. Every now and then, you'll spot the yellow stencilled symbol of the Wilson Trail hiker, apparently dancing the hokey-cokey, to confirm you're still on course.

Strait and narrow: the Lei Yue Mun gap

Look back now across the Lei Yue Mun passage, the narrow gap which separates Hong Kong Island from the mainland. The bright white sails on the opposite headland (above) belong to the Museum of Coastal Defence, built in the former domain of army barracks. The rocky coast below was home to the Brennan torpedo installation, a Victorian invention designed to protect the harbour from foreign warships.

At marker *W021*, you can take a short detour up to the summit of Devil's Peak ('Fortress Mountain' in Chinese), where you'll find extensive ruins of wartime defences. With its strategic location over the eastern approaches to the harbour, Devil's Peak was one of the first places to be fortified after the New Territories were acquired in 1898.

Wartime remnants on Devil's Peak

W024 Rising above the level of built-up eastern Kowloon

Carry on northwards. Down to the east, the meticulously arranged terraces of the Chinese cemetery look out, in accordance with feng shui, over the ever-shrinking expanse of Junk Bay. Carry on along the same contour, the high-rises of Kowloon filling the view to the west. Just short of the barrier ahead, descend the steps to reach O King Road. Bear right for 100 metres then cross over to the pavilion. The trail resorts to stone steps at *W024*, to mount the steep ridge of Black Hill.

You are helped on your ascent by frequent groves of shade-giving trees which offer respite from the sun. As you rise above the level of built-up eastern Kowloon, Lion Rock appears far to the northwest, and the abandoned Kai Tak airstrip stretches out into the harbour. To the east, the new town of Tseung Kwan O steadily grows in size. The old settlement of Rennie's Mill, a ramshackle township inhabited by former Kuomintang soldiers and festooned with Nationalist flags, has completely disappeared beneath the Ocean Shores development.

Descend Black Hill by mud-packed steps, avoiding the first paths off to the left and continuing until the granite marker appears below the pink-coloured

In East Kowloon, a cruise terminal takes
shape on the long-vacated Kai Tak airstrip

W030 Hidden haven: dense, lush greenery well secluded from the city

Chinese pavilion. Continue on by way of the two disused, fenced-in beacons. On the way down, at *W025*, you pass a zoo of grotesque cement figures created by an eccentric artist with a breast-feeding phobia. The trail joins a village track at Ma Yau Tong (Horse Swim Pool) and at the T-junction bears right through the village at *W027*. Cross Po Lam Road at the traffic lights, one of the main entry routes into Tseung Kwan O. Follow Tsui Lam Road until its first fork, turning left at marker *W028*.

W028 Modern-day civic sculptures

This puts you onto another village track, littered with abandoned cars, which peters out into a path at Au Tau. The way ahead is up the staircase.

The remaining stretch to Tseng Lan Shue passes through a lush valley punctuated by repair shops, village houses and barking dogs. The trail reaches the Clearwater Bay Road opposite the poetically named village of Man King Toi: Terrace of Myriad Views. To leave the trail at this point board a bus from the near side of the road for Choi Hung and Diamond Hill MTR stations. Or, if you are tackling the next stage, turn left and take the underpass to the other side of the busy road. Continue, by way of the marble pavilion on your left, until you reach the granite W marker.

Wilson Trail

STAGE

4

Tseng Lan Shue
井欄樹

Tseng Lan Shue 井欄樹 >
Sha Tin Pass 沙田坳

8.0 km / 3 hours

> ### Starting at Tseng Lan Shue

Take the MTR to Diamond Hill and exit to the bus station beneath Plaza Hollywood. Board bus 91, 91M, 92 or 96R. Alight at Tseng Lan Shue village on Clearwater Bay Road, well before the bus reaches the pass and prison at Pik Uk. The trail branches off to the left behind Man King Toi, crossing a stream and plunging into thick forest.

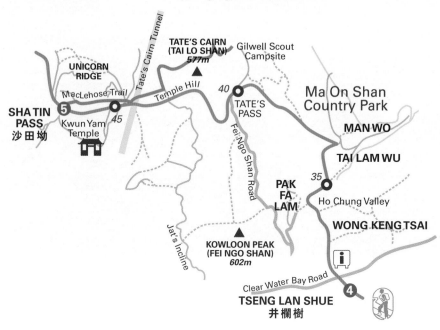

Weave your way through the 'car-repair' village of Man King Toi. As you climb over a gap between two hills, and descend into the luxuriant Ho Chung valley on the other side, glimpses of handsome Kowloon Peak (Flying Goose Mountain) are available through the trees. Here the Wilson Trail offers some of the most desirable hiking conditions in all of Hong Kong. Crossing mountain streams, the path is soon joined from the left by another trail which was the traditional route to Sai Kung before Hiram's Highway was built.

W034 *Forest waters flow freely across the Wilson Trail*

Kowloon hills: Fei Ngo Shan's earthy rampart before the New Territories

Ancient stone route to the eastern coast

The trail joins a village road at the mapboard near marker *W035*. Keeping to this for 500 metres or so, it then turns left and proceeds steeply uphill. The mud path leads up over mossy rocks, fallen leaves and exposed roots, surrounded by impenetrable jungle and the sound of birdsong. Kowloon Peak looms to your left. Suddenly you break out into the open, to be greeted by a wonderful marine panorama of Hebe Haven *W038* and offshore islands spreading at your feet (following spread).

"You are here"

The way ahead leads across the southern slope of One Rise More to meet Fei Ngo Shan Road at the Gilwell Campsite archway at *W040*. Turn left and then sharp right. The road points

Woodland ways. The destination is yours

Flying crested tree lizard

W038 Ports-of-call: Port Shelter and Marina Cove

south as if it is going to mount the ridge of Kowloon Peak, but loops back to head north. At its junction with Jat's Incline, a popular spot for its panoramic views of Kowloon (following spread), markers for the MacLehose Trail appear. Both trails then head west along Unicorn Ridge.

This quiet hill road sees a trickle of one-way traffic, but it's peaceful enough and the views of Kowloon and hazy Hong Kong Island (following spread) are superb. Carry on to Sha Tin Pass, where a well situated café serves the usual egg noodles and cold drinks – or, in the winter months, hot 'dau foo' with syrup – to weary ramblers. Toilet facilities are provided across the road. MacLehose marker *M101* matches Wilson *W046* at this point.

To reach public transport, take the road downhill to your left, passing the entrances to the popular Kwun Yam Temple, until you reach the Sha Tin Pass Estate. Green minibus 18 will carry you to Wong Tai Sin MTR station.

Elephant grass waving in the wind

Rock steady over North East Kowloon

W042 Westward ho toward Lion Rock

On Kowloon's southern horizon Hong Kong
Island fades into the haze

Wilson Trail

STAGE

5

Sha Tin Pass
沙田坳

Sha Tin Pass 沙田坳 >
Tai Po Road 大埔公路

7.4 km / 2.5 hours

> ### Starting at Sha Tin Pass

Take the MTR to Wong Tai Sin and leave by
Exit A. Find green minibus 18 beside the
impressively large temple and ride it to its
terminus on Sha Tin Pass Road. Walk up to
the yellow-roofed monastery and then follow
the minor road all the way up to Sha Tin Pass.
Alternatively you might hail a taxi for a $50
ride to the café on the Sha Tin Pass. To do
so enter the temple compound, mount the
granite steps and take a right up the side
street to the junction with Wong Tai Sin Road.
Taxis frequently pass here. It's an uphill,
winding ride along a route crowded with
early morning hikers.

W049 *Sha Tin's valley stretches northwards to Tolo Harbour*

Kam Shan Country Park

65 **TAI PO ROAD**
大埔公路 **TEI LUNG HAU**

Water Treatment Works

Lion Rock Tunnel Road

Kowloon Reservoir

6
60 Water Catchment

55

Amah Rock

Lion Rock Tunnel

BEACON HILL
457m

EAGLE'S NEST
305m

Sha Tin Tau New Village 50

Lion Rock Country Park
SHAP YI WAT

Unicorn Ridge

MacLehose Trail

LION ROCK
495m

5 **SHA TIN PASS**
沙田坳

The pass is a junction of several roads and footpaths. Our trail leaves the café on its right and heads north over the gap. Stay on the tarmac road headed for Shap Yi Wat; after a few minutes, the trail departs to the right into the trees of Lion Rock Country Park.

The earthen path north is easy walking, and you're offered views of Sha Tin (previous spread) across a foreground of windswept elephant grass. A makeshift shrine on your left is attended by a crew of elderly morning walkers, each comfortably swaying in a hammock swung between the trees.

At marker *W049*, the trail heads sharply downhill by way of a cement staircase to reach the water catchment, and then settles once more for a horizontal course for the following five kilometres until Tai Po Road at *W061*. It's a tranquil environment, particularly if the catchwater is dry, and you shouldn't be surprised if you come across a group of people meditating in silence, legs crossed in the lotus position, at one of the rest pavilions. In many places the quiet is broken only by the crunch of your own boots on the gravel path.

The catchment path is crossed by trails leading up to Amah Rock. Near marker *W054*, one path leads down to Hung Mui Kuk, a convenient and pleasant escape route. (To follow it, take the steps on your right down to Hung Mui Kuk Road, passing through the popular weekend barbecue area. Then take the underpass, and cross over to the bus stop on the opposite side; bus 182 will soon be along to whisk you to the Macau Ferry on Hong Kong Island.)

W054 Day trippers at Amah Rock

To rejoin the trail at this point, take bus 182, opposite the HSBC headquarters in Des Voeux Road Central. Once through the Lion Rock Tunnel the bus will drop one off at its first stop on Hung Mui Kuk Road. On alighting, head briefly in the direction you came from. Behind the apartment blocks the Amah Rock beckons on the horizon. Head for the underpass and take the steps located immediately on the right to The Lion Rock Country Park, clearly signposted.

The Wilson Trail continues along the level contour path, sections of which have been widened and 'shotcreted' beyond what seems necessary. Perhaps the planners are secretly acting in the interests of the armies of macaques inhabiting the jungle on either side, who are now able to march around their kingdom five abreast.

Mind the macaques, they swing in every branch

The trail, under constant repair because of landslips caused by torrential rains, passes a series of picnic areas, and outdoor exercise stations, on its way to join the dangerously busy Tai Po Road opposite the reservoir at *W061*. To leave the trail any bus from the near side of the road will carry you down to Kowloon.

W050-060 Tranquil hiking along the moss-lined water catchment

Trees and water in abundance – great feng shui

Wilson Trail

STAGE
6
Tai Po Road
大埔公路

Tai Po Road 大埔公路 >
Shing Mun Reservoir
城門水塘

5.3 km / 2 hours

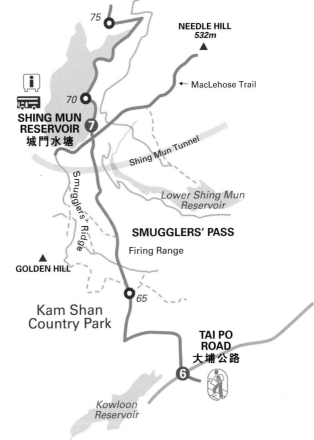

75

NEEDLE HILL
532m

← MacLehose Trail

70

**SHING MUN
RESERVOIR
城門水塘**

7

Shing Mun Tunnel

*Lower Shing Mun
Reservoir*

SMUGGLERS' PASS

Firing Range

Smugglers' Ridge

▲
GOLDEN HILL

65

Kam Shan
Country Park

**TAI PO
ROAD
大埔公路**

6

*Kowloon
Reservoir*

❯ Starting at Tai Po Road

**Take the MTR to Sham Shui Po station
and leave by Exit D2. Walk up Kweilin
Street to Tai Po Road, then head uphill,
passing the Garden Biscuit Factory,
to the bus stop opposite the North
Kowloon Magistracy. Buses 72 or 81
will take you up to the start of Stage
6 at the Sha Tin Heights. Alight after
the parking area on the left, where
Kowloon Reservoir meets the road.
The trail branches off to the left.**

Dragonfly endemic to Hong Kong

Stage 6 commences beside the busy two-lane tarmac road. The first Wilson Trail sign *W061*, is on your left, just before the gate. As you press forward into the greenery of Kam Shan (Golden Hill) Country Park, it's not long before the traffic noise is left behind. You walk a pleasantly shaded path uphill across rushing streams, the sound of water a welcome distraction. Take a right turn at marker *W064* to join the Kam Shan Family Walk.

W066 The trail ahead to Smugglers' Ridge

The trail emerges from the trees onto Golden Hill Road and once again briefly shares tracks with the MacLehose. Watch out for sharp-eyed monkeys, who are accustomed to receiving scraps of food here. Turn right

Tranquil hiking on earthen pathways

on the service road to reach another fork. Off to the right, the existence of a firing range is sometimes announced by gunshots. At *W066* (left), you'll come across a marble tablet commemorating the opening of the following section. Behind it, the Wilson Trail heads up into the trees.

A steep flight of steps leads up to Smugglers' Ridge and views of hills to the east. Turn right from the top to make a knee-jarring descent by stone steps to Smugglers' Pass. The trail leads northwest through thickets of bamboo, and you can look down at the bizarre sight of the Shing Mun Tunnel, traffic popping out of a hole in one hillside to immediately disappear into another.

Two-way traffic hurtles through the Shing Mun Tunnel

The path levels out as you approach the shores of Jubilee Reservoir where, at weekends, barbecue sites are abuzz with the noise of dozens of families. The granite causeway of the main dam lies directly to your right, and this section finishes at its far end.

The quickest way to return to town is to follow the road around the reservoir in the opposite direction, i.e. westwards, to Pineapple Dam and the country parks visitor centre. From there you can board minibus 82 which will take you down to Tsuen Wan and the MTR.

W069 Fishing for the one that got away

Wilson Trail

STAGE
7
Shing Mun
Reservoir
城門水塘

Shing Mun Reservoir
城門水塘 >
Yuen Tun Ha 元墩下

10.2 km / 4 hours

Shing Mun Country Park

YUEN TUN HA
元墩下 ⑧

LO LAU UK

TA TIT YAN

85 ○

Maclehose Trail

LEAD
MINE
PASS

▲
GRASSY HILL
647m

80 ○

SHING MUN
ARBORETUM

Jubilee
(Shing Mun)
Reservoir

75 ○

70 ○

⑦ SHING MUN
RESERVOIR
城門水塘

Shing Mun Reservoir, replenished after the rains

❯ Starting at Shing Mun Reservoir

Leaving Tsuen Wan MTR station by Exit B, take the walkway to Shiu Wo Street to find green minibus 82. At its Pineapple Dam terminus, turn right to walk the often crowded shores of Jubilee Reservoir. After crossing the main dam, turn immediately left. The Wilson Trail is signposted on the granite wall to your right.

Leaving the tarmac road behind, the Wilson Trail stays close to the water's edge. This winding route is shared with the Shing Mun Jogging Trail. For the next 5 km or so, the trail hugs the exposed eastern banks of the reservoir, passing through thick groves of bamboo and crossing mountain streams which rush down the hillsides to empty into the broad, rippled waters. This section offers increasingly rare hiking conditions on natural clay paths, with minimal country parks concrete.

Shing Mun brim full

Paper-bark forest on the reservoir's edge

W077 Cascading white waters after an unexpected downpour

At the northern tip of the reservoir *W077*, the trail joins a cement waterworks road and turns left to follow it to a mapboard near a bridge. The wider streams which join the reservoir here, better named in Chinese than in English as "shek kan" or "stony brooks", are mossy-banked rivulets whose rocky courses provide beautifully refreshing prospects. But they can turn suddenly into pebble-laden torrents after heavy rainfall.

Carry on straight ahead at the meeting of two roads, where there is a mapboard with directions for Tsuen Wan and Tai Po. Villagers would once have walked this route between the two old market towns. The concrete service road now turns away from the water, rising gently through lush woodland towards Lead Mine Pass. A further fork offers a detour to the Shing Mun Arboretum, an open-air haven (opposite) of native tree species which may be the remnants of an old feng shui wood. The Wilson Trail however bears left to make the final ascent: a rise spanning markers *W080 – W083*. Further ahead another 'y' fork requires a decision – take the path straight ahead, to the rest site with toilet facilities at *W083*.

At Lead Mine Pass, well provisioned for hikers with picnic tables and tap water, the trail is once again crossed by the MacLehose, which runs from east to west. Leave the paved road here, beside the public toilet, to descend north via concrete steps towards Tai Po (following spread).

W087 Tai Po at day's end

Markers *W084 — W087* plot a well-trodden descent over a rugged trail partly consisting of rocks and tree roots, fast-paced streams crossing the path at intervals. A swathe of new growth further down is the result of hill fires, usually caused by careless people burning incense during the twice-yearly grave-sweeping festivals. A recent increase in the number of ostentatious, marble-edged 'horseshoe' graves in the area will only exacerbate the problem.

Scorched earth: after Ching Ming

A set of concrete steps lined with heavy metal railings leads down to the village road of Yuen Tun Ha at *W087*, offering views en route in the valley beyond of Tai Po illuminated by the setting sun. A neighbouring village, Ta Tit Yan or Iron-Beating Cliff, perhaps recalls the mining industry which once thrived in the hills above. To break the trail walk down the road to San Uk Ka, where minibus 23K may be picked up for Tai Po Market MTR station.

Picnic retreat in a shady hollow

Water-worn stones

樊仙宮

師靈赫濯扶持合境集千祥

師靈赫濯扶持合境集千祥

信士
馬馳港
來棋元
陳鑑陳
培堅祐
全敬送云

仙像莊嚴護佑通鄉添吉慶

丙辰年仲春月重修開光紀念

仙像莊嚴護佑通鄉添吉慶

W090 Fan Sin temple is open all week, except on Tuesdays

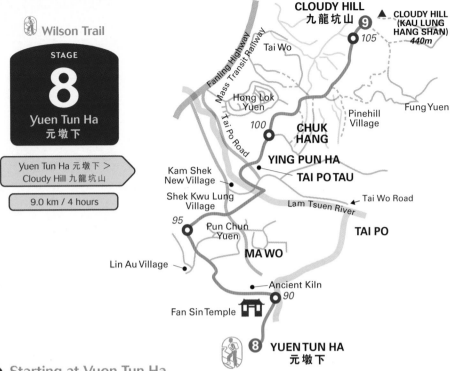

Wilson Trail

STAGE 8
Yuen Tun Ha
元墩下

Yuen Tun Ha 元墩下 >
Cloudy Hill 九龍坑山

9.0 km / 4 hours

CLOUDY HILL
九龍坑山

9

105

CLOUDY HILL
(KAU LUNG
HANG SHAN)
440m

Tai Wo

Fanling Highway

Mass Transit Railway

Tai Po Road

Hong Lok
Yuen

100

CHUK
HANG

Pinehill
Village

Fung Yuen

YING PUN HA

TAI PO TAU

Kam Shek
New Village

Shek Kwu Lung
Village

Lam Tsuen River

Tai Wo Road

TAI PO

95

Pun Chun
Yuen

MA WO

Lin Au Village

Ancient Kiln

90

Fan Sin Temple

8

YUEN TUN HA
元墩下

> Starting at Yuen Tun Ha

Take the MTR to Tai Po Market and jump into a green New Territories taxi for the short journey to Wun Yiu. This outlying village is also served by green minibus 23K, boardable at the minibus terminal adjacent to the station. It's a five-minute ride, buses leaving every 12 minutes and arriving at the village immediately after crossing the bridge.

The trail strikes westwards from the road near Sheung Wun Yiu. Marker *W090* appears at the intersection on your left as you ascend. Take a short detour to the temple of Fan Sin, just beyond the open air carpark on your right, traditionally worshipped by potters. Set in an immaculately swept courtyard shaded by grand banyan trees, it venerates three brothers who were the first to use local clay to make earthenware. The surrounding hills, densely wooded, flowing with

Camouflaged Tokay gecko

water and rich in kaolin deposits, are ideally suited for the porcelain industry which thrived around Wun Yiu from the seventeenth century onwards. In fact the name Wun Yiu itself refers to the kilns used to fire crockery. The well-tended temple is open 9:00-1:00 pm, 2:00-5:00 pm, but closed on Tuesday.

The trail, clearly signposted, carries on through ill-kept banana groves until marker *W092* appears to reassure you of your course. It continues up concrete steps with yellow-painted railings. The rock-strewn path joins more screed and then crosses a makeshift metal bridge over a bubbling stream. From here it follows in the overall direction of Cloudy Hill, passing beneath a line of pylons to join Shek Lin Road, another little-used service track. From here until you reach Tai Po water is a scarcity, unless you take advantage of the leaking water pipe at the side of the road. A little further on at *W094*, an enchanting view unfolds in the valley below: the picture-perfect village of Lin Au, with its

W093 Shoddy plumbing will be fixed – maybe not!

W094 *The mountains are high, and the Emperor is far away from Lin Au village*

tended fields, temple and weekly washing hanging out to dry in the sun. The protective green hills of Tai To Yan rise in the distance to create the impression that you could almost be somewhere in the rural China of classic tradition. Indeed, the village lies in a perfect feng shui setting. Mountains protect its rear, while low hills embrace both flanks. The underlying reasons for such a fortuitous configuration were strategic: offering defence from behind with unobstructed views to the fore of approaching strangers.

In these surroundings, it's easy to appreciate the meaning behind the name of Tai Po; although the characters used have since changed, the original name meant Big Strides, an exhortation to travellers to move quickly through the wooded hills lest they be set upon by tigers.

Bamboo boughs to temple territory

Bear right on Shek Lin Road, to find Pun Chun Yuen at **W096**, a temple situated in tranquil gardens, overshadowed by lush bamboo groves, and attended by black-clad Buddhist nuns. A large silver urn on its balcony holds a forest of lit incense sticks.

The trail from here to the summit of Cloudy Hill is meticulously signposted by the Tai Po District Office. Head on downhill, passing beneath the Tolo Highway to the taxi roundabout at marker **W097** which is somewhat obscured by the greenery beside the pavement on your right at the end of Shek Lin Road. You're now in the ambiguous, half-rural outskirts of Tai Po, an area clacking with the unmistakable sound of mahjong tiles. Walk through Kam Shek New Village, past the colourful children's playground where a little outdoor café serves hot noodles and soft drinks, to the gaudy Kam Wo Bridge. Turn left

W096 *Eaves and leaves greet the rise of a new day*

Golden Buddhas survey the worshipful

The trail snakes through folded hills above Hong Lok Yuen

Crossing the Lam Tsuen River

W099 Red, the colour of joy

'Safe', but not a patch on the former natural beauty

on the other side to walk along the embankment of the Lam Tsuen River. The path soon joins Tai Po Tau Shui Wai Road and then, to the swoosh of trains bound for the border, ducks under the railway line by way of an underpass.

The trail follows Tai Po Tau Drive to the end of the road, passing an ancestral hall – sandwiched between houses at *W099* – which was recently awarded a UNESCO Asia Pacific Conservation Certificate of Merit. On the right hand side is located a convenient pit stop. Then it's back into the green, heading uphill amidst shrubs and bushes. Shiny marker *W100* confirms your bearing. Sadly from here on the trail passes through an area affected by the 'scorched earth' policy of local authorities who apparently have money – as well as vegetation – to burn. The brush from the base to the summit of Cloudy Hill, between markers *W099* and *W105*, has been severely cut back, leaving little shade cover; and the natural dirt path of a few years ago has been 'improved' into a concrete stairway encased by ubiquitous overbearing railings. Remember here to apply sunscreen lotion as the 'improved' concrete path is not only monotonous to hike on, but also raises temperatures and reflects the sun's UV rays upward.

W101 The enclave of Hong Lok Yuen

The path mounts a ridge above Hong Lok Yuen ('Garden of Joy and Prosperity'), allowing birds-eye views of the pools and gardens of the expensive residential enclave at **W101**. The first strenuous climb of this section is now ahead, with rest pavilions en route, as the path scales the southern spur of Cloudy Hill ('Nine Dragon Gullies Mountain' in Chinese, possibly for feng shui dragons descending to nine valleys below). Once at the airy summit, you can enjoy views of the fertile Sha Lo Tung plateau down to the east, a place rich with rare species of dragonfly, which has been fought over by developers and conservationists for many years. The alluvial plain to the west is a patchwork of fallow fields and villages.

This stage ends here beside a rest pavilion at **W105**, amidst the radio aerials on the peak of Cloudy Hill, defying logic and practical considerations of getting home. You must continue on to Stage 9 as far as Hok Tau Reservoir, making your way downhill to Hok Tau Wai to catch green minibus 52K back to the MTR; or take the paved service road all the way down from the peak, skirting the Kau Lung Hang villages and crossing the bridge over the Fanling Highway to catch buses south.

Wilson Trail

STAGE

9

Cloudy Hill
九龍坑山

Cloudy Hill 九龍坑山 >
Pat Sin Leng 八仙嶺

10.6 km / 4.5 hours

> ## Starting at Cloudy Hill

The trail joins the service road at marker *W106* on the summit of Cloudy Hill, and follows it north until it meets a fork and mapboard shelter, there departing to the right and once again treading a dirt track. Lush greenery borders the path along its 200-metre descent to the Hok Tau Reservoir, the lowest stretch down a zigzag stone stairway. After the arduous Cloudy Hill climb, you are rewarded from here on with some of the finest hiking conditions imaginable. Beyond *W107*, at the Country Park shelter, follow the earth path. Where it meets another at *W109*, the dirt path drops down to the right to aim for Hok Tau. The path again turns abruptly right after marker *W113* near the mapboard.

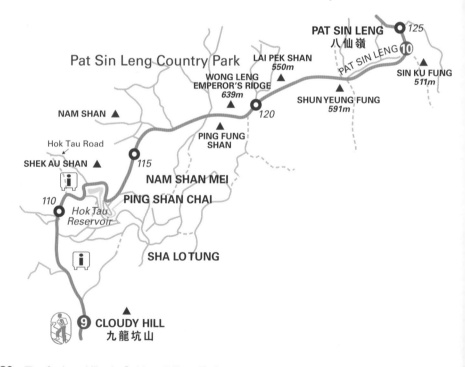

Summits in sequence: The Ping Fung Shan ridgeline

W113 The ever-welcome map board

If you are walking this stage independently of the preceding one, you will need to start by taking the MTR to Fanling and boarding green minibus 52K at the rank near the station. This runs to the rather ancient but still inhabited village of Hok Tau Wai, from where you must walk on a gradual incline up the waterworks road to the reservoir.

The river which is dammed here was known in colonial times as the Jhelum, after a watercourse in the Punjab, but since the British army vacated its New Territories barracks, the river is marked only by its Chinese name on the maps. The Wilson Trail crosses the dam and skirts the pine-shaded northern edge of the reservoir, passing small groups of shoreline fishermen enjoying the peaceful morning. Families are busy planning their day's walk at the "you are here" information boards at *W113*.

Turn left at a barbecue site; the trail heads up across the Hok Tau Reservoir Picnic area through trees to begin the ascent of Hong Kong's most dramatically beautiful range of hills. At this stage be forewarned. It's a point of no return till you reach marker *W126*.

Still waters run deep at Hok Tau

From there it's another hour's hike down, either to Tai Mei Tuk or to continue with the Wilson Trail provided you have enough daylight and energy. Ahead is a beautiful, breathtaking (literally) and strenuous climb with no shade cover, no access to water along the entire Pat Sin Leng ridge. The ascent is steep, up a Gulliver-sized, rock-solid stairway (following spread), and you may need to stop occasionally to catch your breath. Look back as you mount the ridge; the reservoir below is a silver horseshoe set amongst dark forest. Abandoned rice terraces line the lonely slopes to the south. Nearing the top, the trail levels out to loop behind the western end of the ridge. Then, with little warning at *W115*, you stand at the very edge of the awesome escarpment of Ping Fung Shan.

Land drops away almost vertically to the south to reveal an amazing panorama of Tolo Harbour, Plover Cove and the green coasts of Sai Kung. In the opposite direction, foothills march confidently towards the border with China. Tall grasses wave elegantly in the wind.

W115 Like a rumpled green blanket, the hills drop towards the shore

W103 Ascending Cloudy Hill, take a deep breath

Sheltered and secluded Hok Tau Reservoir

Pat Sin Leng in diffused profile

Great divide: the dramatic Ping Shan escarpment

W125 East along the Wong Leng ridge as the sun fades

The trail passes by Wong Leng, the highest point of the range; take the short detour to the top. Its name could be taken to mean Emperor's Ridge; and indeed the views from its summit are commanding. From this privileged viewpoint one is able to see the western and eastern coasts of the New Territories simultaneously.

Ahead to the east, the well-defined trail is clear. At Lai Pek Shan, you stand once more giddily high above the villages of Plover Cove. The final succession of eight humps is known as the Pat Sin Leng, or Eight Immortals Range (left), each peak named after a character of Chinese mythology.

This stage ends atop Sin Ku Fung, the last of the immortals at Marker *W126*. The direct descent to the south is dangerously steep and overgrown; you should take instead the gentler path to the north, turning right onto the Pat Sin Leng Nature Trail at Marker *W013*, to reach Tai Mei Tuk. This waterside village is a fine place for a celebratory dinner. Bus 75K or Minibus 20C will whisk you to Tai Po Market station.

Plover Cove: The dam wall disconnects sweet water from the sea

Pat Sin Leng overlooks the placid Plover Cove

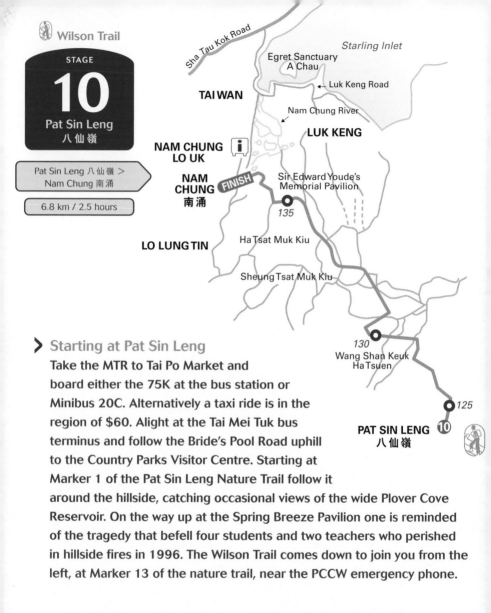

Wilson Trail

STAGE 10
Pat Sin Leng
八仙嶺

Pat Sin Leng 八仙嶺 >
Nam Chung 南涌

6.8 km / 2.5 hours

Sha Tau Kok Road

Starling Inlet

Egret Sanctuary
A Chau

TAI WAN

← Luk Keng Road

Nam Chung River

LUK KENG

**NAM CHUNG
LO UK** [i]

**NAM
CHUNG** FINISH
南涌

Sir Edward Youde's
Memorial Pavilion

135

LO LUNG TIN

Ha Tsat Muk Kiu

Sheung Tsat Muk Kiu

130
Wang Shan Keuk
Ha Tsuen

125

PAT SIN LENG 10
八仙嶺

› Starting at Pat Sin Leng

**Take the MTR to Tai Po Market and
board either the 75K at the bus station or
Minibus 20C. Alternatively a taxi ride is in the
region of $60. Alight at the Tai Mei Tuk bus
terminus and follow the Bride's Pool Road uphill
to the Country Parks Visitor Centre. Starting at
Marker 1 of the Pat Sin Leng Nature Trail follow it
around the hillside, catching occasional views of the wide Plover Cove
Reservoir. On the way up at the Spring Breeze Pavilion one is reminded
of the tragedy that befell four students and two teachers who perished
in hillside fires in 1996. The Wilson Trail comes down to join you from the
left, at Marker 13 of the nature trail, near the PCCW emergency phone.**

As you head north, in lovely hiking conditions with overhead shade on dirt
track with rocks, roots and fallen leaves to negotiate, you cross a sun-baked
landscape of shoulder-height shrubs and bushes; home to quick, low-flying
birds. The nature trail then forks off to the right, and you turn left, descending
into cool, mossy hollows crossed by untamed streams. Water splashes over
stepping stones to make progress hazardous after rainy weather.

Cool, damp woodlands embrace the ancient stone path

W130 Movie sets for haunted woodlands

W135 Memorial Pavilion overlooking Starling Inlet

The long-abandoned villages of Upper Wang Shan Keuk at *W130*, could almost serve as movie sets for haunted woodlands. Shells of empty houses, backed by creaking groves of mature bamboo, seem ready to collapse into the soggy, leafy ground at any moment. The trail continues over Wong Shan Keuk South Bridge, and you'll be pleased to know that there is also a Wong Shan Keuk North Bridge a few hundred metres further along, inscribed in gold lettering.

The stone path crosses further sodden grasslands and seasonal watercourses on its gradual descent over rocks to the well-sited Sir Edward Youde Memorial Pavilion. Dedicated to the governor who died before his time in 1986, while in Beijing to negotiate the terms of the future handover, it sits on a spur overlooking Starling Inlet and the coast of China. It was opened by Lady Youde in 1988, and is a good place to pause to take in the view of sea and mountains. Return the few metres to the signpost. At Marker *W135*, turn left off the stone path, pass the ostentatious gravesites and continue in the direction of Nam Chung.

Pomp and plumage: Sir Edward Youde at his inauguration in 1982

The five villages of Nam Chung in the valley below are each named for the surnames of the original clan inhabitants. The trail winds downhill to join a service road, passing family gravesites which, in this misty hillside environment, are strangely reminiscent of

Gregarious Great Egret

W135 *Verdant valley: Lush lowland at trail's end*

Private paradise: egrets return to their exclusive island

the chortens of Tibet. Then, as you cross the bridge to reach marker *W137*, the Wilson Trail is done. There is no red carpet, no welcoming committee – and unless you have made special arrangements, no celebratory cups of tea served in royal-ciphered Government House tableware from Royal Doulton – just a solitary marker by the side of the road, like the 136 which preceded it, and the sense of satisfaction that you have walked from Stanley to the very edge of Shenzhen, and surveyed the country in between.

Huge boulders mark the course of the river below (previous spread). Follow the road down past the villages of Nam Chung, where black-hatted Hakka women sit outside their houses, to the picturesque temple on the shore of Starling Inlet. En route you'll pass a ramshackle, lean-to stall whose owner offers hot noodles and a welcome shandy. Green minibus 56K pass by to take you to Fanling MTR station. As you travel north to join the Sha Tau Kok Road, look out across the shallow waters of the bay; on their private island of A Chau, you may see hundreds of white egrets settling in for the night.

An overland trip along the Silk Road took **Pete Spurrier** from London to China in 1993, and he has lived in Hong Kong since then, exploring the city's backstreets and hiking its hills. When not bribing sampan ladies to transport him to distant islands, he spends his time deciphering the secret language of minibus drivers. Pete's guided walks have appeared in the *South China Morning Post*, in local magazines, and in *The Leisurely and Heritage Hiker's Guide*, also published by FormAsia Books.

Addendum:

Since the first edition of this guidebook was published, we've been delighted to receive questions and feedback from hiking readers. Much of this has helped us update the guide each time. One query stands out: What to do if you're an overseas visitor to Hong Kong, with perhaps a day or two spare to tread the trails after a business trip or family visit? You are unlikely to know where the free country park campsites are located, or where to buy walking gear, stove gas and other outdoors necessities. With this in mind, we list the following websites as sources of useful information.

Outdoor Specialists:
http://www.chamonix.com.hk/shop.html
http://www.alink.com.hk/
http://www.protrek.com.hk/index.php?lang=en

HKSAR recommended campsites:
http://www.afcd.gov.hk/english/country/cou_vis/cou_vis_cam/cou_vis_cam_cam/cou_vis_cam_cam.html

The Serious Hiker's Guide to Hong Kong

Published by:
FormAsia Books Limited
706 Yu Yuet Lai Building
45 Wyndham Street
Central, Hong Kong
www.formasiabooks.com

Ninth Edition Published 2014
ISBN 978-988-98269-2-5

Text and photographs
©FormAsia Books Limited

Written by Pete Spurrier
Photography by Kwan Kwong Chung/
Sathish Gobinath

Produced by Format Limited, Hong Kong
Design: Alice Yim/Maggie Wan
Digital production: Nelson Pun/
Dickson Chou/Fred Yuen
Maps: Dickson Chou/Edwin Chiu/
Sunny Chan
Production supervision: Jenny Choi

Printed in Hong Kong by
Treasure Printing Company Limited
Images scanned by
Sky Art Graphic Company Limited, Hong Kong

Rights reserved.
Reproduction permitted on written permission of
FormAsia Books Limited.